MAYFLOWER II
Plimoth Plantation

Photography by Ted Curtin
Introduction by James W. Baker

Plimoth Plantation, Plymouth Massachusetts

The Mayflower Story Begins

The *MAYFLOWER* story begins in the small north Nottinghamshire village of Scrooby. In about 1606, a group of English religious dissidents, whom we know as 'the Pilgrims,' formed their own church independent of the national Church of England and its head, King James I. William Brewster, Richard Clifton, William Bradford and John Robinson and their families felt that their Christian faith required a greater degree of church reformation than was possible in the King's established Church. They therefore decided to gather themselves into a church of their own under a separate covenant. Such a move was considered treasonous at a time when church and state were united, and the Separatists, as they were called, were forced to flee the country lest they be imprisoned or even executed for their beliefs. After a disastrous false start at Boston in Lincolnshire – where they were discovered and imprisoned – and a more successful attempt near Immingham, on the Humber River, the little company was able to emigrate by 1609 to the tolerant haven of the Netherlands.

After a brief stay in Amsterdam, where they were dismayed by the discord within other immigrant English congregations, the Pilgrims were granted permission to settle in the cloth manufacturing city of Leiden. They lived there for almost 12 years under the religious leadership of Pastor John Robinson. While they were made welcome in Leiden and found no barriers to the practice of their faith, the Pilgrims still could not find peace and security. Their poverty, as foreigners at the bottom of the economic

ladder, promised hardship in old age. Their living conditions made it difficult for the congregation to recruit additional English immigrants. They feared the loss of their English traditions as their children were growing up Dutch and there was a threat of renewed war between the Dutch and the Spanish. In 1618, the little congregation made the momentous decision to emigrate yet again.

But where could they go? England, their old home, was still closed to them. They discussed settling in South America, but decided that the hot climate would "not well agree with our English bodies". There was also the menace of the neighboring Spanish. On the other hand, the Pilgrims were dubious about joining the English colony of Virginia for fear of suffering religious persecution once again. A later offer to settle under the auspices of the Dutch Government in New Amsterdam was also rejected. In the end they decided to trust their countrymen in Virginia – but at the farthest remove possible. Their goal would be the northernmost boundary of the Virginia Company grant, at the mouth of the Hudson River.

Departure to America

It was not possible to just go to the New World and settle. A patent or license to colonize was necessary and it took a sizable investment as well. The English claim in America, called "Virginia" in its entirety, was divided between two chartered companies which were established to promote settlement and manage the resulting "plantations" or colonies for the English Crown. The London Virginia Company had juris-

A seaman fills a canvas bucket with salt water to wet down the decks in dry weather.

diction over the land from what is today North Carolina to New Jersey, and the Plymouth (Devon) Virginia Company from New York to Maine. In 1618, the Pilgrims began negotiations with the Virginia Company of London, with hopes of getting some assurance from the King that they would be left alone to practice their religion in America. Although the King would not formally promise this, the Pilgrims decided to accept what they viewed as his implicit assent and go ahead with their plans.

The Pilgrims were unable to acquire a patent from the ineffectual Virginia Company of Plymouth. Instead they accepted a patent and permission to settle in the Virginia territory from the London Company. The needed capital to finance the venture was promised by a London merchant, Thomas Weston, who offered to organize a group of "merchant adventurers" (speculators) who would invest the money necessary for a voyage to America. The Pilgrims sent two agents, Robert Cushman and John Carver, to England to work with Weston to prepare for the expedition. The Leiden congregation decided which of the group would go on the first voyage and which would wait until the plantation had been established. They also bought a small 60 "tun" (tun barrels it could hold, rather than tons of water displaced) vessel called the *Speedwell*. The first emigrants left the port of Delftshaven, amid tears, prayers and farewells on July 22, 1620.

The Pilgrim group sailed to Southampton, a city on the English south coast, where they were joined by additional immigrants recruited by Weston and the mer-

chant adventurers on a 180 tun ship out of London, Christopher Jones master. This ship was the *MAYFLOWER*. Following a five week dispute over the contract with the adventurers, the passengers on the two ships set sail for America on August 5. Their voyage was soon interrupted when the smaller *Speedwell* was discovered to be leaking badly. They put into the port of Dartmouth, Devonshire, and repairs were made, but the condition re-occurred once they were under sail again. The two ships were forced to make port a second time, in neighboring Plymouth.

There it was decided to leave the defective *Speedwell* behind, and continue with the *MAYFLOWER* alone. Some of the *Speedwell's* passengers and cargo were transferred to the larger ship, and on September 6, 1620, the *MAYFLOWER* set sail across the North Atlantic and its famous 102 passengers, into history.

The Ocean Crossing

The beginning of the crossing was pleasant "with a prosperous wind which continued divers [many] days together," although many of the passengers were seasick. There then followed a period of many storms and crosswinds, which cracked a main beam in 'tween decks and caused the upper works to leak badly. The conditions were severe enough to raise questions about the capacity of the *MAYFLOWER* to make the voyage. After much debate it was decided to go on as they were nearly halfway across the ocean and the ship was fundamentally sound.

There were only two casualties during the voyage. A sailor (who had greatly har-

Sheltered by a bulkhead on the main deck,
one of the passengers enjoys some fresh air and daylight to sew.

assed the passengers) died before they were half way over, and William Butten, a servant of Samuel Fuller, died just before they sighted land. John Howland came close to being the third fatality when he was swept overboard during a storm, but he was able to seize a trailing topsail halyard and was rescued. There was one birth during the time at sea; Elizabeth Hopkins had a son, who was named appropriately "Oceanus."

Arrival and Exploration

Land was sighted on November 9, 1620. It proved to be Cape Cod, which although the right latitude, was well east of their original destination at the mouth of the Hudson River. However, an encounter the following day with the shoals which lie off the outer Cape, as well as the lateness of the year, persuaded them to remain in the Cape area. The *MAYFLOWER* came to anchor in what is today Provincetown harbor on November 11, after 66 days at sea. That day the male passengers signed the famous agreement we now know as the "Mayflower Compact."

While the *MAYFLOWER* remained in the harbor at the tip of Cape Cod, the people went ashore to shake off the months of travel, to wash their linen and to explore what they perceived to be a wilderness. A shallop – a small coastal craft – had been stowed below decks in sections. The pieces of the shallop were unshipped and brought ashore to be put together. This took 16 or 17 days. While the Pilgrims were waiting for the shallop to be reassembled, sixteen armed men set out on November 15 under the command of Captain Myles Standish to explore the immediate area.

The explorers saw some Native Americans from afar, but were unable to catch up with them. They discovered a buried cache of Indian corn and a kettle, which they took (but paid for the following June), and the remains of a fortification. As they wandered William Bradford was caught in the noose of a deer trap. A second expedition, in which 34 men took part, used the shallop to proceed further along the inner Cape. They found many signs of the native population which had fled at their approach, more corn and the burial of a European man.

Plymouth Founded

It was on a third expedition that the exploring party arrived in Plymouth harbor, where they finally found a suitable place for their permanent habitation. On December 6, ten men braved the frigid winter weather to take the shallop once again along the coast. They found a Native American burial ground and some unoccupied dwellings before camping for the night. At daybreak on December 9, they were attacked by the local inhabitants in a brief exchange of arrows and musket shot, but no one was harmed. The party then proceeded in the shallop only to be caught in a rising storm. First the heavy seas broke the rudder hinges; then their mast split into three pieces. It was all they could do to maneuver the shallop into a nearby harbor and land on an island where they spent a cold and rainy night. The following day being the Sabbath, they did little but explore the island. It was later named "Clark's Island" apparently after Thomas Clarke, the mate of the *MAYFLOWER*.

The sailmaker works on the maintenance of the heavy linen canvas sails.

On Monday, the 11th of December, they went ashore in Plymouth where they found cleared fields and plenty of fresh running water. It was at this time that the famous landing on Plymouth Rock was presumed to have occurred, although there is no record of it in the original accounts. The explorers then returned to the *MAYFLOWER* to say that they had, at last, found a suitable place to build their new community. The *MAYFLOWER* arrived in Plymouth harbor on December 16, 1620, and construction on the settlement began on the 23rd.

The First Winter at Plymouth

The *MAYFLOWER* remained in New England with the colonists throughout the terrible first winter. Although the ship was cold, damp and unheated, it did provide a defense against the rigorous New England winter until houses could be completed ashore. Nevertheless, exposure, malnutrition and illness led to the death of half the group, both passengers and crewmen. There were four deaths (and one birth — Peregrine White) during the month they spent at the tip of Cape Cod. The remainder of the winter saw the deaths of another 40 or 41 colonists. At the lowest ebb, only seven people were healthy enough to tend the sick. On January 14, a fire destroyed the thatched roof on their first structure or "rendezvous" but fortunately none of the sick people that lay within were hurt. A second fire a month later was put out without incident. Despite all of the tragedies and hardships, the Pilgrims persevered in building their new settlement. The village street was laid out with two rows of plots

for their houses and gardens. A platform was erected on the top of the hill above the village, and six cannon installed for defense.

The colonists had observed Native Americans near the settlement in mid-February, but it wasn't until Friday, March 16, that the two peoples actually met. It was then that the famous encounter occurred when Samoset, an Abenaki sagamore from what is now Maine, entered the little village and said "Welcome, Englishmen." Samoset had learned English from the English fishermen who crossed the North Atlantic each year to fish for cod. He told the Pilgrims of the great plague which had killed all of the Patuxet people who had previously occupied the cleared farmland where the new colony sat, and of the ill-feeling the local Native Peoples had towards the English following some kidnappings by Thomas Hunt, an English captain who had visited the area a few years before. During Samoset's visit, the colonists were busy planting their garden seeds.

On March 22nd, Samoset returned with another Native American, Squanto, who was one of the men who had been captured by Hunt. His adventures abroad, from slavery in Spain, escape to London and return to America as a guide in the employ of Sir Ferdinando Gorges, had taught him well about the ways of the Europeans. Squanto, or Tisquantum, became the little colony's chief interpreter and agent in their interaction with the Native Peoples. His arrival paved the way for a visitation by Massasoit, the regional leader among the Native People, the Wampanoag. After an exchange of

A seaman caulks a seam with tarred oakum.

greetings and gifts, the two peoples signed a treaty of peace which would last over fifty years.

Departure of the *MAYFLOWER*

Fields on the south side of the brook were turned by hand and crops of wheat, barley, Indian corn and peas planted in early April. Work continued on the houses. The weather was improving. Spring was in the air and people were recovering from the winter illnesses. The surviving half of the crew were presumably eager to return home, and the colony was ready to bid farewell to the *MAYFLOWER*. The little vessel left New Plymouth on April 5th, and made a quick one month return to England. From there we largely lose sight of the *MAYFLOWER* until she was sold for scrap value after Master Jones' death; 128 pounds, eight shillings fourpence, on May 26, 1624.

Except for the deaths of Gov. Carver and his wife, the arrival of warm weather saw the end of the terrible mortality of the First Winter. During the following summer the little community cared for their crops, came to know their Indian neighbors better and were blessed with a bountiful harvest. They celebrated this tangible indication of survival by holding a three-day celebration after the manner of harvest festivals in England. They invited Massasoit, who came with a retinue of 90 men, and the whole company feasted on fowl the colonists shot and five deer the Indians contributed. It is this event we now identify as the "First Thanksgiving," although it was not an official Thanksgiving in the minds of the participants.

Mayflower II and Plimoth Plantation

Plimoth Plantation was founded in 1947 as an outdoor museum honoring the Pilgrims of Plymouth. A replica of the *MAYFLOWER*, a 1627 Pilgrim Village and a Wampanoag Indian Camp were among the exhibits proposed in the original prospectus. The outdoor exhibits were designed by architect Charles Strickland, and the "First House," a re-creation of the first structure built in 1620, was erected on the Plymouth Waterfront in 1948 to publicize the venture. In 1951, Plimoth Plantation commissioned naval architect William A. Baker to research and design a re-creation of the Pilgrims' *MAYFLOWER*.

The only data about the ship in the contemporary sources was that she had a "burthen of 180 tuns", at least one topsail, and the master's name was Jones. All other information, even the name, had to be found elsewhere. The first time the name *MAYFLOWER* is mentioned in Plymouth Colonial records is in the 1623 land division. Interest in the Pilgrims promoted great curiosity about the *MAYFLOWER* in the 19th century, but her history was complicated by the popularity of the name. There were over twenty ships of that name in the period around 1620. After several mis-identifications (such as the *MAYFLOWER* under the command of William Pierce which brought additional colonists to Plymouth in 1629, or a *MAYFLOWER* with a master named Thomas Jones, which had been a slave ship among other things), R.G. Marsden was able to demonstrate in 1904 that the *MAYFLOWER* in question was out of Harwich and later of London,

The Master was in charge of the ship in the 17th century.
When there was a Captain, he commanded the military personnel, not the vessel.

Christopher Jones, master. It was Christopher Jones who had witnessed the will of William Mullins, which was discovered in the public records at Somerset House in London, aboard the ship in 1621.

The *MAYFLOWER* that brought the Pilgrims to Plymouth was probably built before 1606. Christopher Jones of Harwich, Essex, was in command of the vessel as of August, 1609, and was part owner in 1612. Jones moved in 1611 to Rotherhithe, a shipping center on the south bank of the Thames near London. It was from there that his ship went to Southampton to make the historic voyage.

No picture of the *MAYFLOWER* ever existed, although many speculative artistic representations were made during the 19th century. More accurate research resulted in the R.C. Anderson model of 1925, which Mr. Baker used as a starting point for his design. The original Plimoth Plantation intent was to construct a full size "waterline" model on a concrete slab which would be exhibited at the Plantation site. However, fate intervened in the shape of "Project Mayflower, Ltd.," of England.

Project Mayflower

Project Mayflower was the brainchild of Warwick Charlton, an advertising executive who had been inspired by the Anglo-American cooperation during the Second World War. It became his ambition to commemorate this relationship by building a full scale model of the *MAYFLOWER* which could be sailed across the Atlantic. He founded Project Mayflower, Ltd. to raise the money and construct the reproduction vessel. Project Mayflower approached Plimoth

Plantation in 1955 to see if the museum would be willing to maintain and exhibit a "Mayflower II" once it reached the United States. The Plantation agreed to receive the finished ship upon its completion and extended Project Mayflower the use the Baker plans to build their vessel.

Mayflower II's keel was laid on July 4, 1955, at the Upham Shipyard in Brixham, Devonshire. The ship was meticulously constructed to period specifications, including the use of nine miles of true hemp rigging, 550 square yards of hand-sewn linen canvas sails and solid Devon oak for her timbers. Alan Villiers, the renowned expert on square-rigged vessels was chosen as captain. The hull was launched on September 22, 1956, and by the spring of 1957 *Mayflower II* was ready for her voyage to America. Sailing without any auxiliary power the small ship left Plymouth, England, on April 20, 1957. *Mayflower II* arrived in Provincetown, Massachusetts, (where the first *MAYFLOWER* had made landfall in November, 1620) on June 12 and the next day entered Plymouth harbor amid great enthusiasm. After Project Mayflower had exhibited the vessel in New York, Miami and Washington, Plimoth Plantation assumed both the financial liability and ownership of *Mayflower II* in 1958. Since that time, the Plantation has managed and maintained the vessel as a museum exhibit.

In addition to *Mayflower II* Plimoth Plantation has two outdoor living history sites which interpret life in Plymouth Colony. These are the 1627 Pilgrim Village and Hobbamock's (Wampanoag Indian) Homesite.

Threading a three-sided sail needle with waxed linen thread.

1: The Master of the vessel takes a navigational sighting with the cross-staff. By measuring the angle of the sun over the horizon at noon, the vessel's north-south position (latitude) can be discovered.

2: The *Mayflower's* Master (with cross staff) instructs the Ship's Boy in the use of the Quadrant to find the degree of latitude.

1: The 1606 *King's Colours*, combining the red English cross of St. George with the white cross of St. Andrew of Scotland, is raised on the main-mast.

2: Crewmen break out cargo from the main hold. The cargo on the original *Mayflower* was the furnishings, tools and supplies needed to establish the Plymouth Colony.

3: The Shallop is brought alongside *Mayflower II's* starboard "channel" (chain wale).

1: A seaman attends to the command from above while the helmsman consults the ship's compass. *Mayflower II* is steered with a whipstaff rather than a wheel. The Master's commands are delivered from the half deck above through a conning hatch.

2: The binnacle which stands in front of the helm is designed to contain a pair of compasses and a light to see them by.

3: The crew prepares to raise the anchor using the windlass in the bow of the ship.

1: *Mayflower II* at the State Pier in Plymouth, Massachusetts.

2: A seaman climbs the futtock shrouds into the one of the working tops, which are often mistaken for "crows' nests."

1: The chart room on *Mayflower II*, where the Master or Mate used charts and data from the cross-staff, chip log (not shown) and sand glass to work out their course at sea.

2: The Master's Mate consults a chart of the English Channel.

1: Two seamen haul the main tackle on the foc'sle deck.

2: Looking forward from the half deck as the main sail catches a light wind.

1: A seaman keeps watch near a small breechloading deck gun known as a "murtherer" (murderer).

2: The Gunner fires a salute from a "minion," one of the ship's cannon in 'tween decks.

1: *Mayflower II* under sail.
2: The Master and Master's Mate of the *Mayflower* keep a close eye on the seamen working aloft.

1: The port bow, showing the cathead from which the anchor is raised and lowered, with an anchor lashed to the "channel" (chain wale).

2: A ship's officer rests in his "cabbin" or bunk in the Great Cabin in the stern of the vessel.

3: A sailor serves the Master some wine or beer from a pewter "can" in the Great Cabin.

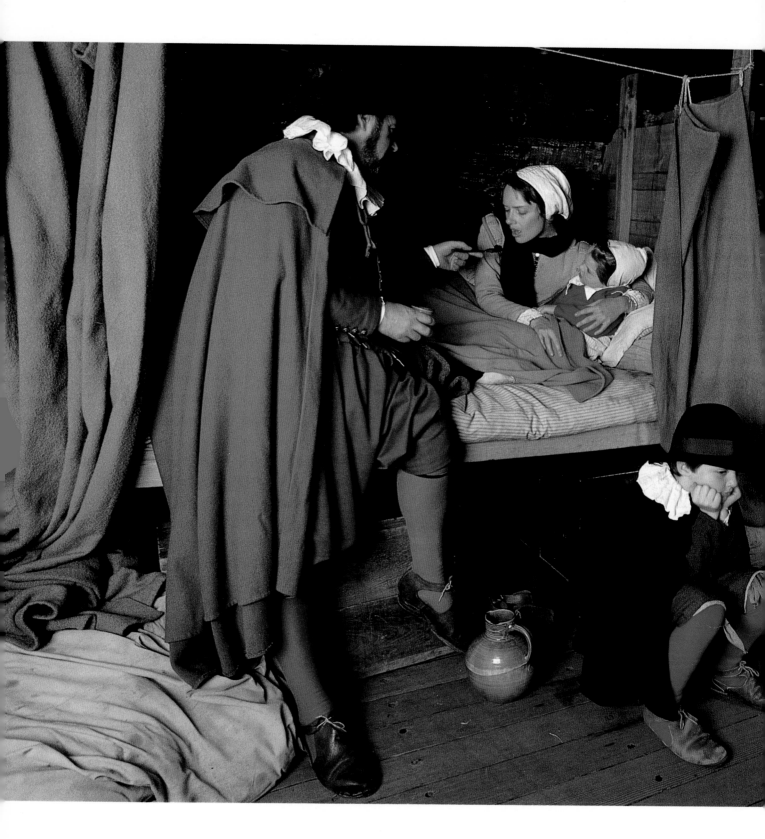

1: Pilgrim families pass their time in their "cabbins" below in the dark of the 'tween decks area.

2: In fair weather passengers were expected to go above decks for exercise and to get away from the unhealthy conditions in their crowded quarters.

3: Mayflower II, accompanied by many small craft, leaves Plymouth harbor to meet two other "Tall Ships", the *Rose* and the *Sir Francis Drake*.

1: Crewmen off-watch take time to rest and play cards in the foc'sle cabin.

2: The helmsman marks the westward progress of the ship by pegging the direction and speed recorded for each half hour of his watch on a "traverse board."

3: Seen from the beakhead a seaman works on the sprit-sail yard.

1: One of the passengers in steerage uses a small charcoal brazier in a box of sand to prepare a meal for her family.

2: The Ship's Cook prepares food for the crew in the fo'c'sle cook room.

3: A crewman ascends the ratlines to work aloft with the sails.

Overleaf: Far above the main deck, a seaman works to correctly furl the foresail.

Crewmen row some passengers ashore
in the 33 foot shallop or workboat.

A fur-clad Wampanoag Indian man smokes a pipe during the hunting season in the winter woodland.

Hobbamock's (Wampanoag Indian) Homesite

Hobbamock's Homesite represents the home of Hobbamock, a Pokanoket Indian who lived with his wives and household (of "above ten persons") on Caughtacanteist or Watson's Hill, south of Town Brook about where Massasoit and Sagamore Streets are today. He was frequently mentioned in the early accounts of Plymouth Colony, and served as the sachem Massasoit's representative to Plymouth as well as acting as a guide, interpreter and advisor on Native affairs for the colonists. Although he tends to be overshadowed in popular history by the better-known Tisquantum (Squanto), Hobbamock had a far longer relationship with the colonists than his rival, who died in 1622. One of Massasoit's pnieses (high ranking warriors and counsellors), Hobbamock lived with the colonists from 1621 until his death sometime before 1643.

The homesite tells the story of the life and times of the most significant resident of Plymouth who did not arrive on a ship, as well as of his family, their people and the greater Native community of southern New England. The re-created site's dominant structure is a "neesquttow," a large bark-covered house appropriate to Hobbamock's social status and family size. The other structures, adjoining cornfield, tobacco garden, storage pits and related features show the daily life of a Wampanoag family living in close proximity to a colonial village. The costumed Native Americans and uniformed staff explain and demonstrate the history and material culture of early 17th-century Wampanoag society.

1: Wampanoag people representing the family of the Wampanoag pniese (counsellor) Hobbamock prepare to construct a bark-covered neesquttow or "two-fire" house. The family corn field and a smaller round wetu lie beyond.

2: A Wampanoag couple trade furs with the Pilgrims for European goods such as linen shirts or cloth coats.

3: Two Wampanoag men enter a wetu – a traditional Eastern Woodland Indian dwelling made of woven cattail mats supported by curved sapling poles.

1: Cargo bales and furnishings to be taken ashore are unloaded from *Mayflower* into the shallop.

2: The shallop, sporting the English *Cross of St. George* flag, makes for the shore. In 1620, the *Mayflower* could not get closer than a mile and a half from Plymouth Rock in the shallow harbor.

A man fires his slow and cumbersome matchlock musket at a fine lot of sitting ducks and geese.

The 1627 Pilgrim Village

Plimoth Plantation's 1627 Pilgrim Village continues the story of the Plymouth colonists that began on *Mayflower II*. The little colony achieved a moderate degree of permanence and prosperity in seven years. The threat of starvation or attack by Indian or Spanish enemies receded, and the community increased to over 150 people following the arrival of three subsequent immigrant ships. The routines of daily life and seasonal cycles of the New World were now familiar. The colony of New Plymouth was ready to expand beyond the town of Plymouth itself.

Plimoth Plantation began construction of the 1627 Pilgrim Village by building four houses in 1957, the same year that *Mayflower II* arrived from England. Since that time the Village has not only grown to include a full complement of family dwellings, a Fort/Meetinghouse, livestock shelters and storehouses, but has also developed an acclaimed first-person living history interpretive program.

When visitors enter the historic area, they are enveloped in the social as well as material culture of the early 17th century. They experience life in an English colony in New England not as an accumulation of craft exhibits and historical lectures but as a living community. Daily life proceeds at a real-time pace with actual work and community activity being undertaken rather than staged activities. Each house, garden and animal pen is maintained in the same way as was done almost 400 years ago.

First-person interpretation places the costumed personnel in the roles of the actual inhabitants of the original village. By using their extensive training, accurate dialects and carefully recreated period mind-sets, they fully replicate the human element of the settlement. Each component of the physical reality of the original village has been re-created as well - for use rather than show. Together the living and inanimate "artifacts" bring the 1627 settlement to life.

1: The Pilgrims harvest a bountiful crop of English grain using traditional methods to reap and bind the sheaves.

2: A young woman uses straw bands to bind the sheaves which will be stored for future threshing.

3: A Pilgrim caps the thatched roof of his clapboarded house with cat-tail reeds.

4: A group of men rive (split) logs to build a defensive palisade around Plimoth Plantation and the Fort/Meetinghouse overlooking the town.

By 1627, the village of New Plymouth had become a successful farming community that maintained English traditions while adapting to New World conditions.

1: A Plantation housewife milks a cow her family shares with others in the community.

2: The men of Plimoth Plantation learn military skills during the annual militia muster.

3: A Plantation housewife tends her frying pan in preparation of the family mid-day dinner.

1: Agricultural activity in New Plymouth slowed down during the cold New England winter.

2: It was the custom in New Plymouth that the parents sit and eat while the children served the meal.

3: Even in the cold of the winter the housewives of New Plymouth had to fire up the community oven to bake their families' weekly supply of bread.

Mayflower II's shallop prepares to come about in Plymouth Harbor.

Acknowledgements

I would like to thank the following people at Plimoth Plantation for their help and support during the production of this book:

To Rachael Montejo, Retail Operations Manager, for developing the project, and for her positive energy and encouragement throughout; to the Research Committee for their enthusiastic endorsement of the project; to Pat Baker and Jill Hall of the Costume Department for their cheerful assistance with last-minute costume calls; to Paul DiSalvatore for piloting the skiff; and to my colleagues Ben Emery, Die Modlin Hoxie and Marie Pelletier for ideas and support. Special thanks to Liz Lodge, Vice President of Exhibits and Maureen Richard, Associate Curator, for the many hours, early and late, spent in preparations for photography, without whose willing assistance my work would not have been possible, and to the members of the Interpretation, Marine Maintenance and Volunteer Departments, who appear in these pictures and bring them to life, for their helpful and enthusiastic cooperation:

Peter Arenstam, Mark Atchison, Scott Atwood, Lucy Baker, Windsong Blake, Kathi Bolt, Stuart Bolton, Jodie Burke, Joy, Roger and Erin Burns, Michael Burrey, Paula Marcoux, Susan Carter, Linda Coombs, Paul Cripps, Rick Currier, Ted A. Curtin, Sandy and Scott Damron, Darrel Dunn, Lawrence Erickson, Kevin Farias, Josh Gedraitis, Tom Gerhardt, Wink Grise, Michael Hall, Bill Ham, Garland Hill, Dahleet Imswiler, Bob Johnson, Kristina Kelly, Susan Kenney, Steve Kocur, Jon Lane, Don Matinzi, Don McIvor, Michael Merritt, Marietta Mullen, Nanepashemet, Bil Orland, Doug Ozelius, Ruud Palenstyn, Sybrejge Palenstyn, Amelia Poole, Reed Remington, Hank Roach, Julie Roberts, George Sampson, Regina Scotland, Marth Sulya, Jonathan Trask, Len Travers, David Walbridge, Annawon Weeden, Lisa Whalen.

I would like to dedicate my work on this book to my parents, Grace and Ted Curtin.

Ted Curtin

Plimoth Plantation, Inc. is a private, non-profit living history museum. It is located 45 miles south of Boston in historic Plymouth, Massachusetts. Established in 1947, the museum has grown from one small recreated house on the Plymouth waterfront to include three major open air exhibits: the 1627 Pilgrim Village, the Wampanoag Indian Settlement, Carriage House Crafts Center and *Mayflower II. Mayflower II* and the Waterfront museum shop are located near Plymouth Rock on the Plymouth Waterfront. The 1627 Pilgrim Village and the Wampanoag Indian Settlement are three miles south on Route 3A at Plimoth Plantation. Support facilities available at the Plimoth Plantation site include orientation theaters, dining areas, gift shops and exhibition galleries.

Photography, unless otherwise noted, is by Ted Curtin.

Edited by James B. Patrick

Designed by Donald G. Paulhus

Published by Fort Church Publishers, Inc., Little Compton, R.I. 02837

Printed in Japan